j973
J.0496
M992c

W9-DGF-524

ONE MORE RIVER TO CROSS

WILDER BRANCH LIBRARY
7140 E. SEVEN MILE RD.
DETROIT, MI 48234

SEP - - 2000

WALTER DEAN MYERS

Harcourt, Inc.

San Diego   New York   London

ONE MORE RIVER TO CROSS

An African American Photograph Album

WILDER BRANCH LIBRARY
7140 E. SEVEN MILE RD.
DETROIT, MI 48234

Copyright © 1995 by Walter Dean Myers

All rights reserved. No part of this publication may be reproduced
or transmitted in any form or by any means, electronic or mechanical,
including photocopy, recording, or any information storage and
retrieval system, without permission in writing from the publisher.

Requests for permission to make copies of any part of the work
should be mailed to: Permissions Department,
Harcourt Inc., 6277 Sea Harbor Drive,
Orlando, Florida 32887-6777.

Photograph credits appear on pages 153–166.

First Harcourt Paperbacks edition 1999

*A special thanks to Michael Farmer and Lydia D'moch
for their contributions in the design of this book.*
—W. D. M.

The Library of Congress has cataloged the hardcover edition as follows:
Myers, Walter Dean, 1937–
One more river to cross: an African American
photograph album/by Walter Dean Myers.
p.   cm.
1. Afro-Americans—Pictorial works.   I. Title.
E185.M97   1995
973'.0496073—dc20   95-3839
ISBN 0-15-100191-X
ISBN 0-15-202021-7 pb

B D F H J K I G E C

Printed in Singapore

The display type was set in Sophia.
The text type was set in Garamond 3.
Color separations by Bright Arts, Ltd., Singapore
Printed and bound by Tien Wah Press, Singapore
This book was printed on Arctic matte paper.
Production supervision by Stanley Redfern and Jane Van Gelder
Art direction by Michael Farmer
Designed by Lydia D'moch

To Donna and Steven Taylor:

Let their works praise them.

INTRODUCTION

THIS BOOK IS A PORTRAIT OF THE PEOPLE OF African descent in the United States. It is not the only possible portrait, but it is one that I believe has not often been seen.

The differences between our people's experiences and those of people of other heritages are striking, but so are the similarities; yet the points of confluence are frequently overlooked. We are often depicted as either exotic or passive, a people who are acted upon but who seldom take control of our own lives. Some portraits of African Americans, meant to be sympathetic, tend to depict us primarily as victims.

The pictures gathered here show our struggles but also our joy and the sense of communion we experience in family gatherings, in religious services, in music, in holiday celebrations. Hard work has always been part of our heritage—and there are photographs of workers—but so has the enjoyment of life. So I've included scenes rarely offered as part of the black experience: happy young women in bathing suits, a college football team, a handsome young man at a military academy. Here are people being people, unburdened by the historical restrictions of race, defining themselves according to *their* understanding of who they are.

Being black in America has not been easy. Considerations of race have always been an integral part of our nation's fabric, and for us this has meant obstacles. There was slavery; then there were the Jim Crow laws, and the ugliness of segregation. Today, preconceptions about race create more subtle obstacles.

Yet the obstacles are also part of our heritage. It seems that no matter how far we have traveled there is always another trial, always one more river to cross. But the adversity of our lives has made our moments of joy that much sweeter, our gatherings that much more meaningful. And that joy and that sweetness have flavored our lives and our contributions to modern America: our labor, our music and poetry, our understanding of a common humanity, our genius.

The variety of black life will surprise many people. Pilots, scientists, gunslingers, dancers, ballplayers, artists—we have been all these things and more.

There were African Americans who had accumulated great wealth by the end of the Civil War. After the war, some who migrated west formed their own towns and prospered. Others built up their own communities in white towns, only to see them attacked by irate mobs, their wealth taken by force, their homes burned. There were black farmers and black college graduates and blacks who were wealthy enough by the turn of the century to travel back and forth to Europe.

There were rivers to cross, but we crossed them. Sometimes it was only one person, a giant such as Frederick Douglass, or the writer and activist Ida B. Wells. Sometimes they came in groups, such as the Tuskegee fliers or the Negro baseball leagues. Sometimes, as in the March on Washington or the civil rights boycotts, they came by the thousands, and even hundreds of thousands. The most amazing aspect of our lives in the United States is that in the face of the myths of underachievement and the constant stereotyping of blacks as being narrow in purpose and restricted in ability, we have participated in everything that this country has offered— and more often than not, we have made important contributions.

These are easy words to write, an easy argument to make, but the truth is that many people today, black and white, have accepted a distorted view of black life. This is understandable considering the way the story has been told—more specifically, considering what has been left out. When America told the story of pioneers moving westward, it spoke of white Americans only. When America told the story of the building of this nation, it told of white workers. It wasn't until quite recently that many Americans even knew that African Americans fought for the Union in the Civil War. We did fight in the Civil War, and in the Revolutionary War, and in the War of 1812, and in the Spanish-American War, and in the First World War, and in the Second World War, and in Korea, and in Vietnam, and in the Persian Gulf.

Finally, the fullness of our story is being discovered. One way this has come about is through photographs brought forth from dusty archives, from attics, and from family albums. Some of these images have been made by professional photographers, others created by amateurs with small box cameras. They were not all that difficult to find; I have thousands of photographs in my own collection. There are collections at many of our major universities, museums, and libraries, at the Library of Congress and the National Archives, at places like the Schomburg Center for Research in Black Culture in New York, and in many other private institutions. The rich, diverse lives of African American men, women, and children, long "invisible," are there to be discovered by those willing to search them out, and especially by those who have enough awareness of our history to understand what they see.

Photographs remind us of what has been. They say: this person or these people have been here. When we look at a family album we not only think of the people in the portraits, we feel the weight of their lives as well. We are reminded of the inner strength that allowed them to hold their heads high, that kept them going on. We are reminded of their daring, their belief in themselves, and their conviction that it was within their ability to triumph. And we need to be reminded so we can call on that same inner strength that exists in us today.

In putting this album together I have not attempted to tell *the* story of African Americans or to include every person who has significance in our history. I think of it instead as only one of the possible stories of this, my extended family.

—*Walter Dean Myers*

ONE MORE RIVER TO CROSS

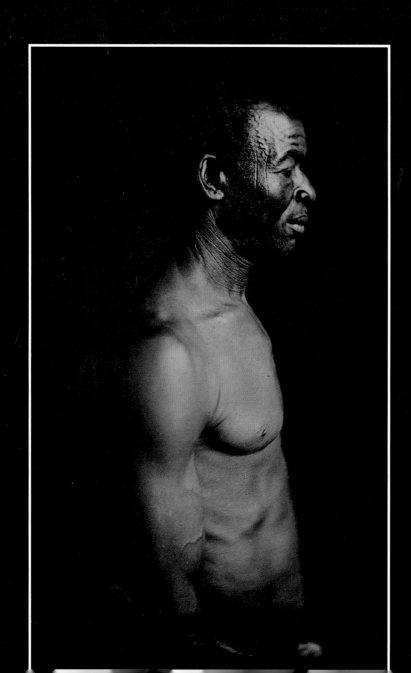

Lord knows

that first crossing was hard.

So many lives, so many dreams

were lost in the foam of that dark ocean.

It hurts the soul just to think about it.

It was hard, but most of us

came through it,

holding on to our faith

that there would be

a better day

somewhere.

We were a strong people. Strong bodies, strong spirits.

From can to can't,

from sunup to sundown,

we did the work

that had to be done.

The sowing and the reaping.

The building up and the cutting down.

The digging and turning of the soil, the grinding . . .

We did it all.

Some of us found freedom early. Not many, mind you,

but when we got loose from the chains and from the whips

we found our *dignity.*

For most of us freedom

was just a dream.

Ranaway,

ON the 10th January last, a Negro Fellow named *MOSES*—he is a likely fellow, about 20 or 21 years of age.— He was purchased of Mr. James White, out of the Work-house, and is well known about town as formerly the waiting-man of Theodore Gaillard, Esq. A reward of *Fifty Dollars*, with all reasonable expences, will be paid on delivering him to the Master of the Work-house, by

JOHN PLATTS, *Barnwell District*, or D. LEITCH, 283 *King-street.*

N. B. If *Moses* will return of his own accord he will be forgiven.   ‡   August 24.

We shed a river of tears

on those plantations

and on those

auction blocks—

bitter, bitter tears.

When the war came

and we had the chance to be

strong

out loud, our men took it.

Men used to bending and bowing

showed they knew how to stand

tall.

Then that hard war was over

and *freedom* came,

freedom came

pouring down

like a sudden

summer rain,

warm and so sweet

to the taste.

We were walking down the streets with

a freedom walk.

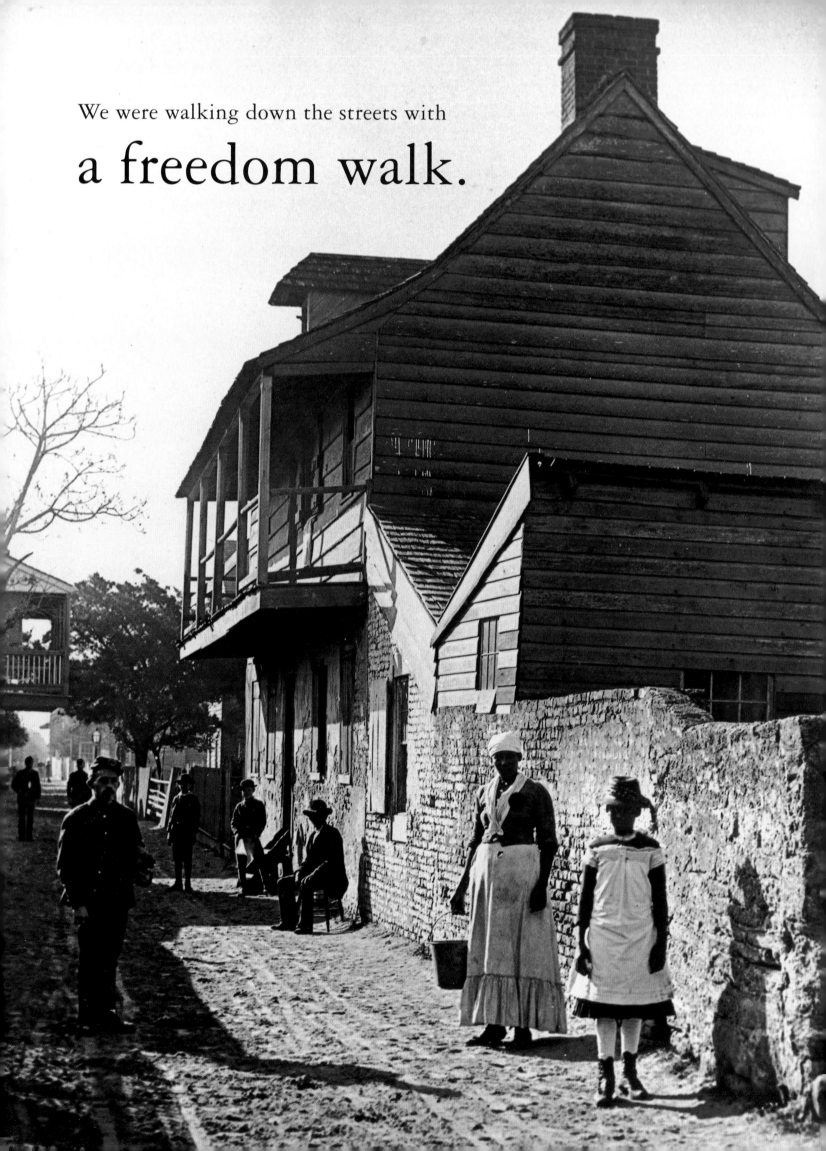

Working was easier

with freedom by our side.

Folks who had

learned to read

started teaching

those who hadn't.

Folks who had run off to freedom started to come back home.

Oh, we still did the work.

But hope had come over the horizon,

hope stood bright on the hill for all of us to see,

and we gathered in joy and called out our greetings

and shouted,

"AMEN, HOPE!

What took you so long?"

We had hope,

but we didn't forget.

No, nobody was forgetting.

Nobody expected it easy.

We were not an easy people.

We had been deepened by the suffering we had known.

We were deep, like the rivers we had crossed.

No, we didn't even need easy.

And there were always the
children.

They were our victory.

We moved away from the darkness of captivity,

making our own way,

and bringing

love and learning

to our children.

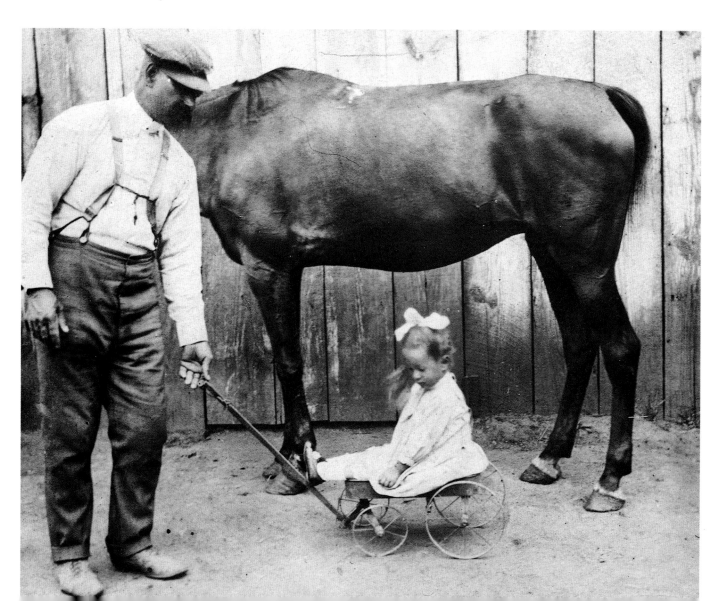

We got on with the work.

And encouraged our *young people.*

We had
the quiet wisdom
of the *elders*
to guide us.

The old warriors,
who had seen so much,
passed their vision
down to the young ones.

And at the center of it all were the families.

We were a hundred different kinds of people,

doing every little thing you could think of,

and some things
you'd never think about at all.

We did **every kind** of work.

Folks were proud to earn their own way.

We saw ourselves as

a serious people,

going about

the serious business

of life.

*We knew
how to wait
for tides
and how
to run them.*

How to remember old wounds . . .

and how to forgive them.

But where we saw families growing up,
some folks only saw *differences,*

and didn't like it.

Where we saw new foundations,
some folks only saw *color*.

Where we saw

heroes

and

scholars,

some folks

just saw us

as being in their way.

Some folks told us what they wanted us to be.

Some folks didn't seem to see us at all.

And didn't

understand

that they

JUST

DIDN'T

UNDERSTAND.

But we just kept keeping on.

Doing what had to be done.

Now, the children of folks

born on plantations,

the children of people

who were beaten and sold,

these children were showing

everyone what free people could do.

The mothers had worked the fields,

but just look at what

their daughters

were doing!

Strange how

some people

could look down

on our

women.

And our men,

strong and deep-rooted

as trees planted
by the river of life.

We couldn't always agree on the path,

but we would go forward.

And we did go forward . . .

doing it all.

Of course,

we had some fellows

with no more

character

than a humpbacked

rattlesnake.

But that's the way life goes, and you have to expect that.

4448

Name, William R Saunders.

Alias,

Crime, Larceny

Age, 26   Comp., Negro.

Height, 5 3 3/4   Weight, 130

Hair, Blk   Eyes,

Nose,   Face,

Marks, Scar left cheek + back left hand. Gold upper tooth

Born, Chester, Pa.

Married, No

Trade, Gambler

Date of Arrest, Oct. 20/97

Officer, McKinley, Div 5

Remarks,

7486

We were *enjoying* ourselves,

living clean and tasting
the fruits of our labor.

We even started our own **communities,**

our own little towns.

pushed down, and beat down,

We knew

what being

strong

was about.

So we just

kept about the business

of who we were.

We weren't all doing good.

Some of us were

struggling

just to make it

from day to day,

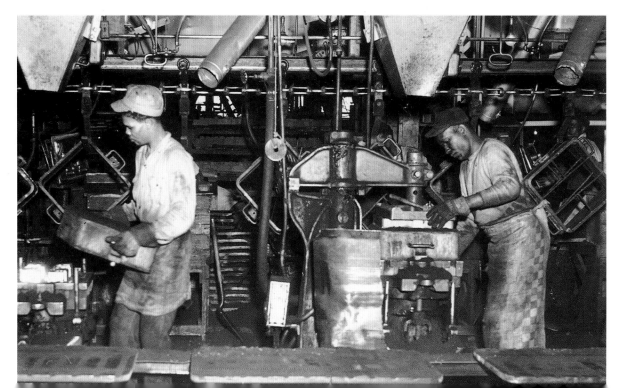

The *variety*

in our lives

was something else.

Look at these young women.

Got a mule hooked up to a car axle.

Isn't that something?

Folks will make do when they have to.

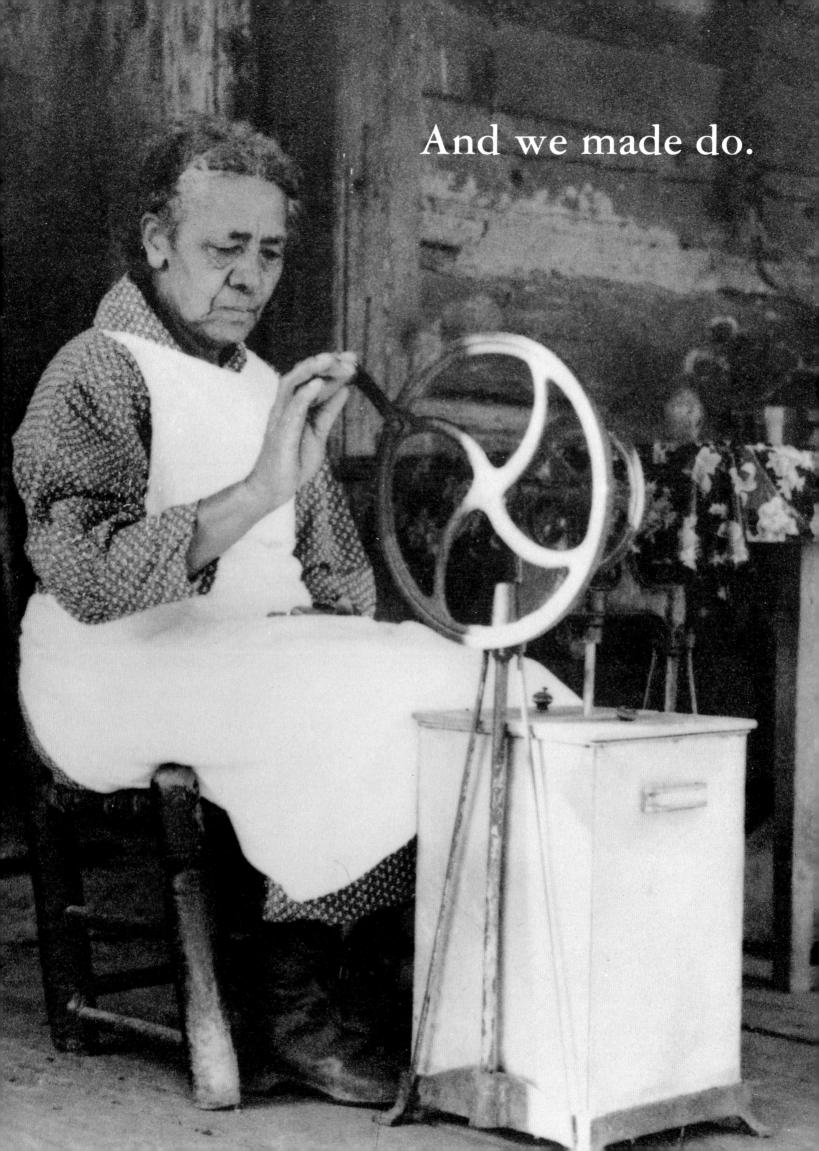

And we made do.

Of course, we were believers, *strong believers.*

It was a belief fired in the forge of hard times

and tempered in the cooling waters of hope.

No matter how we tended

to our own business,

we couldn't forget

what some folks

thought about us.

And the people who

hated us because of our color

WERE PROUD OF THEIR HATE.

Our *roots* were in the South.

We had pulled weeds

in places like

Cross Creek, Georgia,

and Killeen, Texas,

and Mars Bluff, South Carolina,

and all

those little places

where people

knew your name

and who

your family was.

Child, *you know what hard work is?*

It's a farmer

scratching

in the hard earth

looking for a better life.

But when the banks don't want to know you,

you can't get a fair price for your crops,

and you just don't feel safe in your own home,

you reach a point . . .

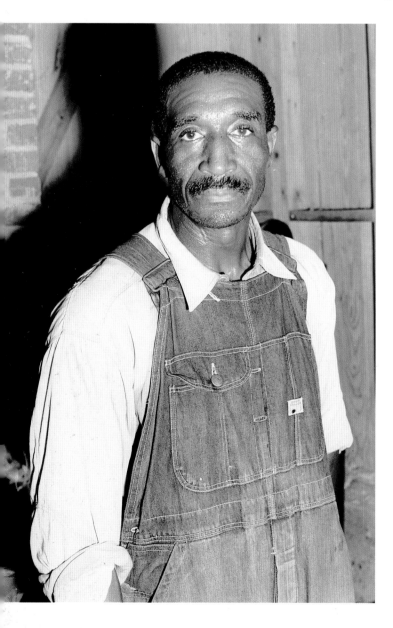

Many of us headed north for a new start.

It wasn't all that we'd hoped for.

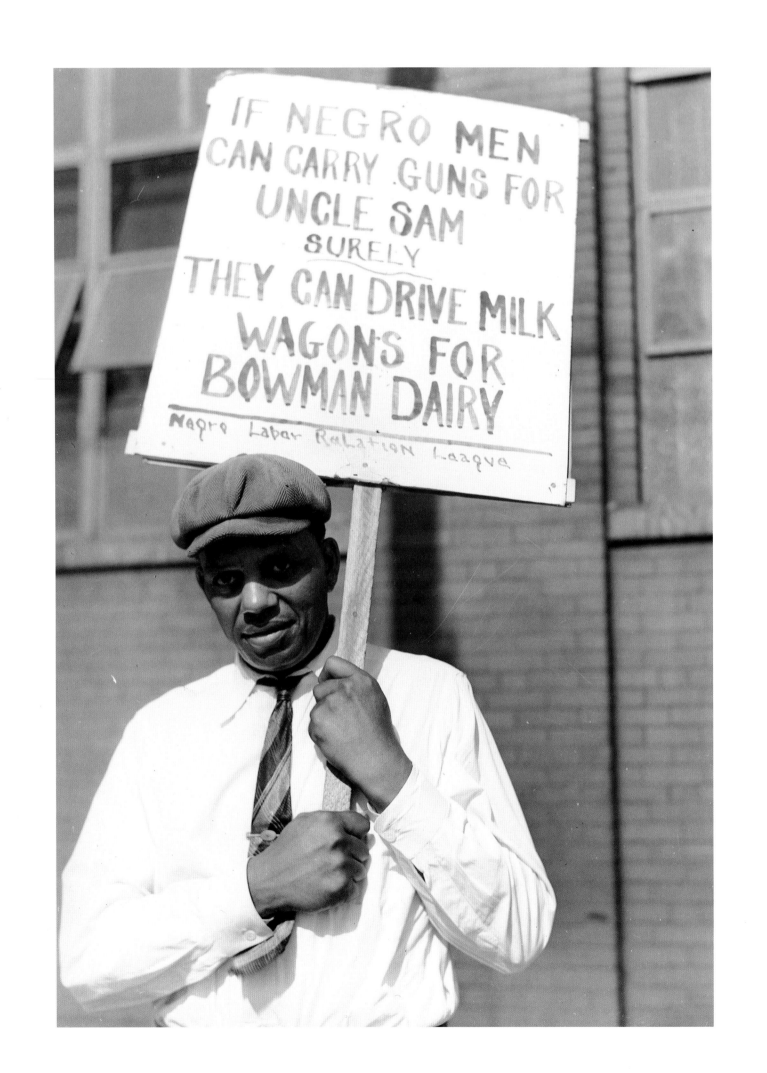

Again we made do.

We brought a *style* to the cities,

*a **swing** of the hips,*

a **rhythm** *that*

folks around the world

began to notice.

And we were still a spiritual people.

Maybe it was

just our time

for a new kind

of strength.

Maybe coming together like that,

listening to one another,

and seeing what we could do up close

brought out the light in us.

Just let it shine on out.

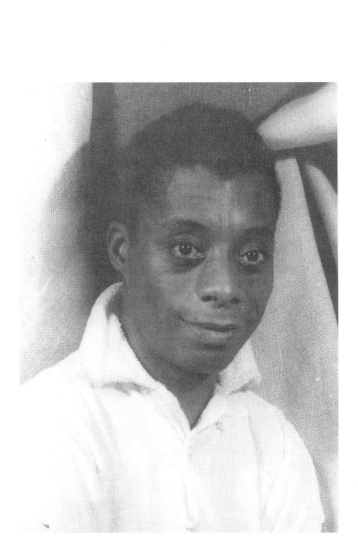

Another war came

and our men lined up with the rest.

He came along

and stole our hearts.

We lived and breathed

that man.

When he got through,

some of us felt

we had all got through,

and we wondered

why

it had taken so long.

It had taken so long and still we had to struggle.

There were people to *lead* us,

people willing to take us to the mountains.

He has delivered my soul in peace from the battle that was against me . . .

Yes,

and we have crossed the rivers

that needed to be crossed,

and have seen the still waters.

Our tears have been washed away,
allowing us to see with our eyes
the stories that have been told

and with our hearts the ones yet to come.

And through it all there is the *sweet triumph of life,*

a triumph we have nourished

like a sacred flame through

the centuries.

We have kept it safe

in southern fields

and northern tenements,

in the western mountains

and through all the rivers,

great and small,

that we have crossed.

The story is of triumph and endurance

and of the breadth and the depth

of the human spirit.

The reason for the story,

for the celebration of what has been,

is that the journey continues.

And truly,
it has been
a powerful journey.

CAPTIONS

Not all the photographs in this book can be accurately dated; nor is it always possible to know exactly where a picture was taken or even why. Many of the images in the author's collection have been recovered from discarded family albums, lost photographers' files, and other sources. The images remain; the history must be reconstructed.

All photographs not otherwise credited are from the collection of the author.

PAGES 2–3

Jack, Guinea driver. An enslaved African from Guinea, West Africa, he was used to supervise other African workers—thus the "driver" designation. Plantation of B. F. Taylor, Columbia, South Carolina, 1850. Daguerreotypes taken by J. T. Zealy as part of a series showing African "types." *(Peabody Museum of Archaeology and Ethnology, Harvard University)*

PAGES 4–5

(Left) Omar ibn Said. Like many of the Africans brought to this country, Omar ibn Said was Muslim. This contradicted the common belief that the Africans were "heathens," a people without their own culture—one of the justifications for the slavery system offered by plantation owners. Said was born about 1770 and died in 1864. Captured in West Africa and brought to Charleston, South Carolina, in 1807, he was an educated man who could write in Arabic. Photograph from daguerreotype. *(Southern Historical Collection, Library of the University of North Carolina at Chapel Hill)*

(Right) Rice workers riding a barge near Georgetown, South Carolina. Rice was grown in West Africa in the area commonly known as the Grain Coast. The skills of these Africans were often advertised by slave traders.

PAGE 6

Woman with hoe. Photograph by Rudolf Eickemeyer, Jr. *(Library of Congress)*

PAGE 7

Cotton-field workers. The labor-intensive work of the cotton fields helped to perpetuate the slave system.

PAGE 8

Clara Brown. Held in bondage for the first fifty-five years of her life, Brown traveled west to Colorado, where she started a laundry business and invested in real estate. She left an estate worth more than ten thousand dollars. *(The Denver Public Library, Western History Department)*

PAGE 9   Affluent man in top hat. Despite the handicaps of racial barriers and slavery, Africans often prospered by virtue of their intelligence and hard work. As early as the mid-eighteenth century, some enslaved Africans were earning enough money to buy their own freedom, and free Africans, such as this man, were accumulating wealth. Ambrotype.

PAGE 10   Slave auction house, Richmond, Virginia. The buying and selling of humans became a business that could be found in every major southern city. *(Library of Congress)*

PAGE 11   Runaway advertisement from the *Charleston Gazette,* 1820. Although slaveholders tried to portray slavery as a paternalistic system and a happy experience for the Africans involved, notices such as this told a different story.

PAGE 12   *(Left)* Sgt. Lewis Douglass, son of Frederick Douglass. He served in the Fifty-fourth Massachusetts Infantry Regiment. *(Moorland-Spingarn Research Center, Howard University)*

(Right) Civil War soldier on guard duty. *(Library of Congress)*

PAGE 13   Sgt. Henry Stewart, Fifty-fourth Massachusetts Infantry Regiment. Stewart was active in recruiting for the regiment but died of disease after the Battle of Fort Wagner. The fight for freedom was joined by Africans from the plantations, by those who were free in the United States, and by many who had escaped to Canada. *(Massachusetts Historical Society)*

PAGE 14   Fallers House, Cumberland, Virginia, 1862. Many Africans made their way to freedom during the Civil War. These people, often still legally "slaves," were called contraband. *(Library of Congress)*

PAGE 15   Family group in front of a plantation outbuilding in Tuckahoe, Virginia. The end of the Civil War and the freedom it brought allowed Africans who had been enslaved (and who now had been made Americans by the Fourteenth Amendment to the Constitution) to enjoy real family life for the first time. *(Valentine Museum, Richmond, Virginia)*

PAGES 16–17   *(Left)* Children at waterfront.
(Right) Family traveling by oxcart.

PAGE 18   Black city neighborhood. In the cities blacks were often restricted to the less desirable properties, but quickly began to build these areas into thriving communities.

PAGE 19   Woman pounding rice in front of a cabin. Cultivating rice was a skill that many Africans had passed down from generation to generation.

PAGE 19 *(cont.)*   The women in this picture are using the same methods employed by their distant relatives in western Africa. Photograph by Rudolf Eickemeyer, Jr. *(Library of Congress)*

PAGES 20–21   *(Left)* Charlotte Forten, 1864. Her grandfather James Forten, who fought in the Revolutionary War, later became a wealthy sailmaker in Philadelphia and a leading black abolitionist. Charlotte Forten, educated in New England, went south during the Civil War to help begin the process of educating the freed Africans. African Americans understood that they were identified as a people and rarely as individuals. Forten, like many educated black people of her day, felt a responsibility to help in the education of other blacks. *(Moorland-Spingarn Research Center, Howard University)*

(Right) Hundreds of blacks had fled to Canada to escape slavery. This group, the Fisk Singers, photographed circa 1870, often sang in communities along the border to raise money for Fisk University.

PAGES 22–23   Peanut pickers display the day's harvest. Prior to the Civil War southern blacks were controlled by the laws of "ownership." After the war they often found that they were trapped by menial jobs and low wages.

PAGES 24–25   Lumber camp workers, circa 1880. African Americans were often hired because they could be paid less than their white counterparts. But the work, and the dignity that came with it, was still welcomed.

PAGES 26–27   *(Above left)* Photograph of older man sitting on a stump, circa 1870. *(Below left)* Western couple. *(Nebraska State Historical Society)* *(Right)* Woman by window. Photograph by Rudolf Eickemeyer, Jr. *(Library of Congress)*

These people, who had spent much of their lives in slavery, now faced spending their remaining days in poverty.

PAGES 28–29   *(Left)* Colorado mine worker and his wife, circa 1870. The need for labor in the West provided opportunities for African Americans that didn't exist in the South. Blacks sought out jobs that did not depend on the whims of a white employer. Mining was hard, and the living conditions were so difficult in these camps that employers took anyone they could get. *(Courtesy, Colorado Historical Society. Copyright 1901 by B. W. Kilburn)*

(Right) Group of women and children in Memphis, Tennessee. Memphis's large black population worked toward self-sufficiency, even as the Ku Klux Klan was being formed there.

PAGES 30–31   *(Left)* Portrait of young girl. *(Above right)* Group of schoolchildren and their teachers in Nebraska. The struggle for education had begun. Blacks understood that education meant opportunity. *(Great Plains Black Museum, Bertha Calloway Collection)*

PAGES 30–31 *(cont.)* *(Below right)* Workers stemming tobacco leaves in Virginia. In some southern communities there were no permanent schools for black children. Instead, the state or county hired black teachers, who traveled throughout a fairly wide geographic area, renting space in churches or homes and conducting classes for periods as short as three months. *(Valentine Museum, Richmond, Virginia)*

PAGE 32 *(Above)* Group of women in front of a house used to store corn. *(Below)* Storefront on Main Street in Richmond, Virginia, circa 1880, decorated to celebrate Emancipation Day. African Americans celebrated different emancipation days, depending on when they had been freed or when they discovered that they had been freed. June 19th, or "Juneteenth," was one of those days. *(Valentine Museum, Richmond, Virginia)*

PAGE 33 Woman walking with boy playing with a hoop toy. The families that came out of slavery were often not "traditional" ones. Birth parents and children may have been sold away from one another and new relationships formed. These extended families may have consisted of a grandmother and grandchildren; sometimes friends agreed to be "family" for one another.

PAGE 34 *(Above)* Portrait of two children in Salina, Kansas. *(Below)* Man and child at a blacksmith shop.

PAGE 35 Black schoolroom. Early black schools were places of serious study, in which teachers and children recognized the value of education.

PAGES 36–37 Georgia quarry workers, circa 1880.

PAGE 38 *(Above)* Henry O. Flipper. Despite constant harassment, Flipper became the first African American to graduate from West Point, in 1877. *(Special Collections, United States Military Academy Library)*

(Below) John Jasper, preacher. Jasper was born on the Fourth of July, 1812, in Virginia. He preached in Richmond, using the metaphors of the destruction of Pharaoh's army and the Israelites' escape to Canaan to bring hope to his black congregation. Clergymen were becoming increasingly important as leaders within the black community. *(Valentine Museum, Richmond, Virginia)*

PAGE 39 Old woman with book and picture.

PAGE 40 Frederick Douglass and his grandson Joseph. Douglass was a self-educated man and a compelling speaker and writer. Born in 1817, he escaped from slavery and was an outspoken leader in the fight to free his people. He personified the difference between white and black abolitionists in

PAGE 40 *(cont.)*   his militant stance and his call for immediate emancipation. After the Civil War, he continued to campaign ardently for black social equality at a time when white abolitionists had abandoned the cause of human rights. Douglass's death in 1895 left a major gap in black leadership. *(Library of Congress)*

PAGE 41   Black family. The basic unit of African American life became the family. In addition, social and religious traditions strengthened black communities to the point where many competed with white communities in talent and wealth.

PAGE 42   *(Left)* Well-dressed couple with dog, Keokuk, Iowa.
(Right) Myers family, Martinsburg, West Virginia, circa 1918.

PAGE 43   Young family, Boston.

PAGES 44–45   Black women and white charges. The women, who were often referred to as "Mammy," worked in all areas of the country. An irony of segregation in the United States was that many whites entrusted their children to black caretakers.

PAGE 46   Diane Fletcher, black Kiowa woman. Black and Indian unions are seldom discussed in history books but were quite common. *(Western History Collections, University of Oklahoma Library)*

PAGE 47   Nat Love. There were many African American cowboys. In fact, up to 20 percent of cowboys in the West were black or Indian. In 1869 Love worked in Dodge City, Kansas. By 1890 he was out of the cowboy business and working as a porter on a Pullman train. *(Library of Congress)*

PAGES 48–49   Pizaro Medicine Show. Even during the time of slavery, whites used black musicians for dances, shows, and promotions. This picture was taken after Emancipation.

PAGE 50   *(Above)* Interior of the John W. Matthews Barbershop. There were many barbershops and hair parlors owned by blacks, but they could not openly serve black customers if the owners wanted to maintain their white business. *(Western History Collections, University of Oklahoma Library)*

(Below) Logging workers.

PAGE 51   Cotton market, Montgomery, Alabama. Years after slavery had ended, many blacks were still tied to cotton.

PAGE 52   *(Above)* Jubilee Singers. In the nineteenth century the music of African Americans was appreciated the world over. These musicians toured

PAGE 52 *(cont.)* Europe and raised money for the struggling black colleges back home. In the process they introduced the world to black spirituals and folk songs. *(Below)* Portrait of mature woman.

PAGE 53 Portrait of young woman, Nashville, Tennessee.

PAGE 54 Portrait of riverboat pilot. Many skilled jobs, such as that of a riverboat pilot, were lost to African Americans as the United States became a more segregated society. On the plantations during the period of African bondage, blacks had been carpenters, smiths, mechanics, etc. Restricted job and training opportunities put new limitations on the black community and made it more dependent on whites. This issue was later addressed by Booker T. Washington.

PAGE 55 Woman and child. *(Oregon Historical Society, #CN022273)*

PAGE 56 Portrait of black family. From the mid-eighteenth century there had been middle class blacks in the Northeast. By 1900 there was a black middle class throughout the country.

PAGE 57 Dry goods store in Red Bird, an all-black town in Indian Territory. Blacks who had been enslaved prior to the Civil War now owned and operated their own businesses, most often in their own communities, thus avoiding direct competition from whites. *(Western History Collections, University of Oklahoma Library)*

PAGE 58 *(Above)* Matthew Henson (1866–1955). Henson traveled to Nicaragua and later to the North Pole with the Peary expedition, in 1909. His work with Peary was largely ignored by the white press, and it was only through the intervention of President Taft in 1913 that he was able to get a job as a messenger with U.S. Customs. *(Library of Congress)*

(Below) George Washington Carver (1864–1943). Carver was a major researcher in soil preservation and a teacher at Tuskegee Institute from 1896, when he headed the School of Agriculture, until his death. In 1931 he refused an invitation by Joseph Stalin to manage the cotton plantations in the southern USSR. Carver was named a fellow of the Royal Academy of England in 1916. Image by P. H. Polk, a black photographer.

PAGE 59 Jack Johnson. Outspoken and defiant, a brilliant fighter, Johnson personified the fears that some whites had of blacks. He won the Heavyweight Championship of the World by defeating Tommy Burns in 1908. The subsequent search for a white champion exemplified the discomfit that some whites felt at black successes. *(Library of Congress. Copyright 1909 Ono Sarony Co., New York)*

PAGE 60   George Walker, Bert Williams, and Ada Overton Walker, black minstrels, circa 1900. Blacks were often not allowed to appear onstage in white theaters unless they did so in blackface; thus, they were denied the opportunity to present themselves with dignity. Instead, they had to act like comical buffoons, fulfilling the stereotypical roles assigned to them.

PAGE 61   Blacks in service occupations, waiting on table.

PAGES 62–63   Family group with household maid and child.

PAGE 64   New England family with early bicycle, circa 1900.

PAGE 65   *(Above)* Woman washing clothes. Doing laundry provided steady income for many families when there were few opportunities for other work.

                 (Below) Madame C. J. Walker at the wheel of a car with Alice Kelly, Lucy Flint, and Anjetta Breedlove, Madame Walker's niece, circa 1912. Madame Walker started her own beauty products business and became the first African American woman to earn a million dollars. Blacks have always done well wherever there were businesses in which the opportunities have been limited only by ability. *(Photographs and Prints Division, Schomburg Center for Research in Black Culture, The New York Public Library, Astor, Lenox and Tilden Foundations)*

PAGE 66   Woman on beach with camera.

PAGE 67   *(Above)* Ida B. Wells (1862–1931). Wells was one of the most outspoken fighters for civil rights of her time. She was also one of the first to use the boycott as a strategy for securing racial justice. *(Photographs and Prints Division, Schomburg Center for Research in Black Culture, The New York Public Library, Astor, Lenox and Tilden Foundations)*

                 (Below left) Portrait of woman.

                 (Below right) Bessie Coleman (1896–1926). Coleman considered aviation to be one of the keys to the future; she believed it was her duty as a black woman to learn to fly. A former beauty parlor worker, she went to France to attend flying school and became a stunt pilot and entertainer. Photograph from the cover of an invitation to a flying show in 1926. *(From the Eartha M. M. White Collection, Thomas G. Carpenter Library, University of North Florida)*

PAGE 68   *(Above)* Paul Laurence Dunbar (1872–1906). Dunbar was a friend of the Wright brothers and an outstanding poet who began the literary tradition of celebrating the lives of the African American working class. *(Library of Congress)*

                 (Below left) Portrait of mature man, Jamestown, New York.

                 (Below right) Bass Reeves, Deputy U.S. Marshal under Judge Isaac

PAGE 68 *(cont.)*   Parker at Fort Smith, Arkansas. Reeves began his career in 1875 and continued to work as a lawman until illness forced his retirement in 1909. *(Western History Collections, University of Oklahoma Library)*

PAGE 69   Soldier, circa 1910. After the Civil War many young men sought opportunities in the army. Black soldiers were called Buffalo Soldiers by the Indians because of their woolly hair and dark skins. They were often used to suppress the western Indian population. *(Collection of Dr. Joseph N. Williams)*

PAGE 70   *(Left)* Blacksmith, Tenth U.S. Cavalry. This black regiment fought during the Indian campaigns in the West, in the Philippines, and in the Spanish-American War in Mexico.
(Right) Soldiers, Tenth U.S. Cavalry.

PAGE 71   Sailors on USS *Herbert,* late 1920s. The *Herbert* saw service in both world wars. The army and navy have traditionally been a source of opportunity for the lower classes of all nations.

PAGES 72–73   *(Left)* W. E. B. Du Bois, circa 1926. A prominent intellectual and social theorist, Du Bois helped form the National Association for the Advancement of Colored People. *(Photographs and Prints Division, Schomburg Center for Research in Black Culture, The New York Public Library, Astor, Lenox and Tilden Foundations)*

(Right) Booker T. Washington *(middle)* on one of his last visits to New Jersey, in 1914. Washington believed that the lower economic classes would advance by improving their job skills and training. Du Bois, on the other hand, stressed intellectual development, which, he argued, would free all people to make their greatest gains. The two men often clashed, as Washington appeared to be willing to promote job skills at the expense of social progress and integration.

PAGES 74–75   *(Below)* Coleman Industrial Home Band, Pittsburgh, Pennsylvania.

(Above) Major Taylor. A professional bicycle racer, Taylor was an outstanding athlete from 1896 through 1915. After he beat most of the white professional racers, they tried to ban him from the sport. When blacks were successful, they often encountered racism that targeted their success. Here Taylor is pictured with another professional racer, Eddie McDuffee. The purse was the equivalent of a year's salary.

PAGES 76–77   William R. Saunders.

PAGES 78–79   *(Left)* Women on beach.
(Right) Men and women cyclists. *(Courtesy, Colorado Historical Society)*

PAGES 80–81 *(Above)* Women on porch.
(Below) Men in hunting party, circa 1915. As more and more blacks, such as these men, became successful, opposition to their success grew. The Ku Klux Klan became more entrenched, even in northern cities, and segregation laws were hardened.

PAGES 82–83 *(Above left)* Homesteaders. Moses Speese and his family, near Westerville, Custer County, Nebraska, 1888. *(S. D. Butcher Collection, Nebraska State Historical Society)*

(Below left) Postmaster and others in front of a post office in the all-black town of Littig, Texas, not far from Austin. Towns like Littig were often developed in order to avoid racial hostility. *(The General Commission on History and Archives, The United Methodist Church)*

(Right) Mr. Mosely in front of his store, Cincinnati, Ohio, circa 1917. Despite segregation and racism, black businesses prospered.

PAGE 84 Black community under attack in Tulsa, Oklahoma, 1921. *(The General Commission on History and Archives, The United Methodist Church)*

PAGE 85 Blacks being moved from their homes during the Chicago race riots, 1919. When the First World War ended, black soldiers returning from the fighting began to migrate from rural areas to cities. The increased competition for jobs exacerbated the racism that already existed, resulting in hundreds of attacks against blacks. *(The General Commission on History and Archives, The United Methodist Church)*

PAGE 86 *(Above)* Woman, Tennessee, 1929. Although legal slavery had ended, many people, including this woman, who lived not far from the plantation on which she had been born into slavery, were still doing badly. But the hard times had given her the strength she needed to survive, and the knowledge of what she had been through helped her to maintain her pride.

(Below) Tony Thompson, photographed in the 1930s. Thompson was born into slavery. *(Library of Congress)*

PAGE 87 Viney Dean. Here Dean starts her day's work in South Carolina. Photograph by A. Wesley Carpenter. *(Carpenter Collection)*

PAGE 88 Mining camp family, circa 1932.

PAGE 89 *(Above)* College football team.
(Below left) Young miners, circa 1932, with firelit headgear, usually worn to light the way in the mines.
(Below right) Two women having fun, circa 1932.

PAGE 90 *(Above)* Men near locomotive.

PAGE 90 *(cont.)*   *(Below)* John C. Robinson (second from right, standing), known as the Brown Condor, an early aviation pioneer. In the 1920s Robinson built and flew airplanes and ran a flying school in Chicago. In the late 1930s he helped Haile Selassie's small Ethiopian air force fight against the Italians. Robinson died in a plane accident in Ethiopia. *(Mrs. Bertha C. Stokes {née Robinson}, private collection, Gulfporians, Inc.)*

PAGE 91   Young men dancing for handouts from tourists at the Hermitage Plantation near Nashville, Tennessee, 1929. While tourists came to see what remained of a large slaveholding plantation, many of the descendants of the people enslaved on that plantation were still doing poorly.

PAGE 92   *(Above)* Logging workers.
(Center) Fishermen, North Carolina. Photograph by A. Wesley Carpenter.
(Below) Foundry workers, Albion, Michigan. In 1916 black workers were brought to Albion from the Deep South by truck to work in the foundries. *(Albion Historical Society)*

PAGE 93   *(Above)* Students at Meharry Medical College, a traditionally black school in Nashville, Tennessee, circa 1919. Colleges in the South were not integrated.
(Below) Rodeo rider, late 1930s. *(African American Museum and Library at Oakland)*

PAGE 94   Depression-era vehicle. While the Depression was hard on both whites and blacks, it had a more prolonged effect on African Americans and served to harden the position of segregationists. Photograph by R. B. Hoit.

PAGE 95   Woman churning butter, North Carolina. Photograph by A. Wesley Carpenter. *(Carpenter Collection)*

PAGES 96–97   Baptism, South Carolina. Photographs by Doris Ulmann. *(Photographs and Prints Division, Schomburg Center for Research in Black Culture, The New York Public Library, Astor, Lenox and Tilden Foundations)*

PAGES 98–99   *(Left)* Theater ticket for segregated seating. Segregation and the feelings of inferiority it created were a burden that African Americans had to bear. Yet, the most significant effect of segregation was not social but economic. By controlling what blacks could and could not do, what education we could receive, and where we could live, whites reduced black competition for jobs, wealth, and positions of power.

(Right) Segregated cafe in Belle Glade, Florida, 1945. *(Photri, Inc.)*

PAGES 100–101   Ku Klux Klan march in Washington, D.C., 1925. *(Library of Congress. Underwood & Underwood, Inc.)*

PAGE 102 — Although both blacks and whites were lynched, this act of mob rule was more frequently directed against African Americans. Whites who carried out the lynchings were not prosecuted, and the entire black community became victims of the terror that lynching inspired.

PAGES 104–105 — Black-owned restaurant in the South.

PAGES 106–107 — Max Killie beside a photograph of himself during World War I, Heard County, Georgia, circa 1940. Many blacks believed that their loyalty and willingness to fight for their country would promote racial justice at home. It did not. *(Library of Congress)*

PAGE 108 — Grandma Lawrence, Greene County, Georgia, 1941. Photograph by Jack Delane. *(Library of Congress)*

PAGE 109 — Farmer, circa 1940. This picture was one of thousands commissioned by the Farm Security Administration to record the lives of farmers and their families during the hardships of the 1930s and 1940s. *(Library of Congress)*

PAGE 110 — *(Left)* Farmer, circa 1940. *(Library of Congress)*
(Right) Older farmer, circa 1940. Photograph by Arthur Rothstein. Farmers were dependent on bank loans and a free market to succeed. Black farmers were denied both. In the 1930s it became increasingly clear that the black family's hopes for the future did not lie in the South. *(Library of Congress)*

PAGE 111 — Married couple prepared for the journey north, circa 1930. Thousands of blacks, convinced that racism would prevent their success in the South, began what has been called the Great Migration to northern cities.

PAGE 112 — City tenement. Every immigrant group that arrived in the cities of the North endured tenement life. Blacks were the only group confined to the tenements by racial identification. Photograph by G. D. Olmstead. *(Photographs and Prints Division, Schomburg Center for Research in Black Culture, The New York Public Library, Astor, Lenox and Tilden Foundations)*

PAGE 113 — Men in front of Harlem apartment house, 1930s. *(Photographs and Prints Division, Schomburg Center for Research in Black Culture, The New York Public Library, Astor, Lenox and Tilden Foundations)*

PAGES 114–115 — *(Left)* Alley dwellers, Washington, D.C. *(Library of Congress)*
(Right) Harlem youth, 1930s. *(Photographs and Prints Division, Schomburg Center for Research in Black Culture, The New York Public Library, Astor, Lenox and Tilden Foundations)*

PAGE 116   Picketer, Harlem. *(Library of Congress)*

PAGE 117   *(Above)* Men listening to radio in Harlem, 1930s. *(Photographs and Prints Division, Schomburg Center for Research in Black Culture, The New York Public Library, Astor, Lenox and Tilden Foundations)*

(Below) Harlem street scene showing office of the United Negro Improvement League, Marcus Garvey's militant organization. Garvey believed that the black man had to establish economic security as a requirement for social advancement. He proposed a "back to Africa" movement, by which he meant not so much a physical return to Africa as an emotional connection with all people of color. *(Photographs and Prints Division, Schomburg Center for Research in Black Culture, The New York Public Library, Astor, Lenox and Tilden Foundations)*

PAGE 118   Bert Williams. A great comic actor, Williams was reduced to playing minstrel roles in the theater. The roles paid well, but the cost in self-respect was high.

PAGE 119   The Gay Northeasterners (a social club): three fashionable women in Harlem. *(Photographs and Prints Division, Schomburg Center for Research in Black Culture, The New York Public Library, Astor, Lenox and Tilden Foundations)*

PAGE 120   Dorothy, Chicago showgirl, circa 1935. *(Standard Photo Service)*

PAGE 121   *(Above)* Josephine Baker. Born in East St. Louis, Illinois, Baker was a stage star by the age of fifteen. *(Culver Pictures)*
(Below) Jennie, Chicago showgirl, circa 1935.

PAGE 122   New Orleans nuns, circa 1930. *(Library of Congress)*

PAGE 123   Members of the black Jewish community in Harlem. The charter to build a synagogue in Harlem was granted by the Falasha Jews of Ethiopia.

PAGE 124   *(Above)* Harlem Renaissance writers *(left to right)*: Langston Hughes, Charles Spurgeon Johnson, E. Franklin Frazier, Rudolph Fisher, and Hubert T. Delaney, circa 1924. *(Courtesy of Regina M. Andrews. Photographs and Prints Division, Schomburg Center for Research in Black Culture, The New York Public Library, Astor, Lenox and Tilden Foundations)*

(Below) Mary McLeod Bethune, educator and civic leader. Bethune started her career in Florida in 1904 and went on to become the director of Negro affairs for the National Youth Administration in Washington, D.C., during the 1930s. *(Library of Congress)*

PAGE 125   Group of elderly ladies, 1925. Photograph by James Van Der Zee. *(© Donna Van Der Zee)*

PAGE 126   *(Above)* Billie Holliday, blues singer. This picture shows her at the height of her career, in the 1930s. *(Culver Pictures)*
(Below) Louis Armstrong, jazz musician. *(Culver Pictures)*

PAGE 127   Marian Anderson. Born in Philadelphia, Anderson sang in her church choir before starting a career of recitals. She later became an internationally known classical singer. *(Culver Pictures)*

PAGE 128   Duke Ellington, composer. *(Culver Pictures)*

PAGE 129   *(Left)* James Baldwin, writer, circa 1930. *(Carl Van Vechten Collection, Library of Congress)*

(Above right) Joe Louis, World Heavyweight Boxing Champion. *(Culver Pictures)*

(Below right) Paul Robeson, as he appeared in Eugene O'Neill's *The Emperor Jones*. Robeson was an actor and singer in the 1920s; in the 1930s he became a political activist. Both Armstrong and Robeson came to manhood during the period of the "New Negro," the first generation of blacks whose parents had not directly experienced slavery. In the major cities black artists were expressing their own culture. Jazz was beginning to be known throughout the world. *(Culver Pictures)*

PAGES 130–131   Negro League All Star Team, 1939. Blacks played organized baseball with whites until the major leagues were formed; then they were banned from major league play. The all-black teams often played exhibition games against major leaguers and also played with them in Mexico. *(National Baseball Library & Archive, Cooperstown, New York)*

PAGES 132–133   *(Left)* World War II soldier.
(Right) Tuskegee Airmen. The armed forces were segregated during World War II, with blacks relegated chiefly to menial jobs. After many protests a flying school was installed at Tuskegee, Alabama. These fliers served their country well in the skies over Europe. *(Photri, Inc.)*

PAGES 134–135   Jackie Robinson. Every black man, woman, or child who did well bore the burden of representing all African Americans. Robinson was selected in 1947 to be the first Negro player in the major leagues (there were other Negro players in professional baseball before Robinson but not in the modern major leagues) because of his ability to handle himself both socially and athletically. *(Culver Pictures)*

PAGES 136–137   March on Washington for passage of the Civil Rights Act, 1963. *(Photri, Inc.)*

PAGES 138   Malcolm X, 1963. *(Michael Ochs Archives–Venice, CA)*

PAGE 139   Martin Luther King, Jr., and Coretta Scott King. *(Photographs and Prints Division, Schomburg Center for Research in Black Culture, The New York Public Library, Astor, Lenox and Tilden Foundations)*

PAGE 140   Soldier in firefight in Vietnam, 1974. *(Photri, Inc.)*

PAGE 141   Soldier crossing water in Vietnam, 1974. *(Photri, Inc.)*

PAGE 142   Family portrait, circa 1930.

PAGE 143   Children at play, circa 1969.

PAGE 144   *(Above)* Schoolchildren, circa 1930.
              (Below) Studio portrait of child.

PAGE 145   *(Above left)* Child in city playground, 1930s.
              (Right) Two children, 1930s.
              (Below left) Three Nebraskan children. *(Great Plains Black Museum, Bertha Calloway Collection)*

PAGE 146   *(Above)* Children, circa 1970.
              (Below left) Studio portrait of child, 1900s.
              (Below right) Child in park, 1977.

PAGE 147   Child on front stoop of apartment house, 1970.

PAGE 148   Child on city street, 1970.

PAGE 149   *(Above left)* Studio portrait of girl, 1890s.
              (Above right) Child with stuffed animal, 1930s.
              (Below) Jackie and Nora Jones dancing on apartment balcony, 1976.

PAGES 150–151 Silhouette of father and son. Photograph by A. Wesley Carpenter. *(Carpenter Collection)*

WILDER BRANCH LIBRARY
7140 E. SEVEN MILE RD.
DETROIT, MI 48234